D1031875

LIFE CYCLES
Oak Trees

by Melanie Mitchell

first step nonfiction

Lerner Publications Company · Minneapolis

This is an **oak tree.**

Oak trees can grow
very big.

How do oak trees grow?

Oak trees grow from seeds
called **acorns.**

Some acorns are planted.

Others just fall to the ground.

First the acorn grows **roots.**

Next it grows a **stem.**

It grows into a small tree.

The tree grows bigger and taller.

Many years later, the tree
makes **flowers.**

Acorns grow from the flowers.

Oak trees must be very old
to grow acorns.

The acorns fall to the
ground.

Animals eat some of the
acorns.

The rest grow into new oak trees.

Life Cycle of an Oak Tree

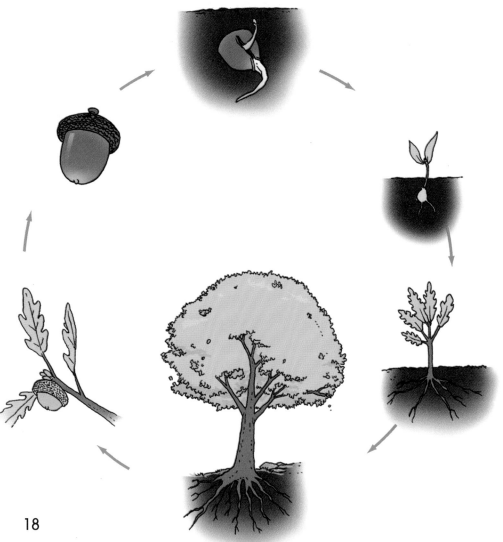

Oak Trees

Oak trees grow all over the world. There are almost 300 kinds of oak trees. Different kinds of oak trees grow in different places.

Oak trees grow very slowly. It takes many years for an oak tree to grow big enough to produce acorns. Oak trees produce acorns in the fall. Some oak trees produce thousands of acorns. Only a few acorns will actually grow into trees and continue the life cycle of an oak tree.

Oak Tree Facts

 Oak trees can live for hundreds of years. A famous oak tree in Maryland called the Wye Oak lived for over 400 years. It was destroyed by lightning in 2002.

 Some oak trees are 50 years old before they produce acorns.

 An average oak tree sheds about 700,000 leaves each fall.

Oak trees seem to be struck by lightning more than any other kind of tree.

 Connecticut, Georgia, Illinois, Iowa, Maryland, and New Jersey all have an oak tree as their state tree.

 The bark from the cork oak tree can be peeled away and used to make corkboards, shoe soles, and insulation. The tree regrows its bark in about nine years.

Glossary

 acorns – the seeds of an oak tree

 flowers – the parts of plants that make seeds

 oak tree – a tree that makes acorns

 roots – the parts of plants that grow down into the soil

 stem – the supporting part of plants that grows above ground

Index

animals – 16

flowers – 12, 13

roots – 8

seeds – 5

stem – 9

The photographs in this book are reproduced through the courtesy of: © Corbis/Royalty Free, front cover, p. 14; © Karlene Schwartz, pp. 2, 3, 13, 15, 22(middle); Todd Strand/IPS, pp. 4, 6, 11; USDA Photo, pp. 5, 22(top); © Photodisc/Royalty Free, p. 7; © Dwight Kuhn, pp. 8, 9, 10, 22(second from bottom, bottom); Minneapolis Public Library, pp. 12, 22(second from top); © G. Rodriguez/Photo Network, p. 16; © Chad Ehlers/Photo Network, p. 17.

Illustration on page 18 by Tim Seeley.

Lerner Publications Company
A division of Lerner Publishing Group
241 First Avenue North
Minneapolis, MN 55401 U.S.A.

Website address: www.lernerbooks.com

Library of Congress Cataloging-in-Publication Data

Mitchell, Melanie S.
    Oak trees / by Melanie Mitchell.
        p.   cm. — (First step nonfiction) (Life cycles)
    Summary: A basic overview of the life cycle of an oak tree.
    ISBN: 0–8225–4610–8 (lib. bdg. : alk. paper)
    1. Oak—Life cycles—Juvenile literature. [1. Oak. 2. Trees.]
    I. Title. II. Series.
    QK495.F14 M58 2003
    583'.46—dc21   2002004870

Manufactured in the United States of America
1 2 3 4 5 6 – JR – 08 07 06 05 04 03